Archaeology
and
Ancient Cultures

UNCOVERING THE CULTURE OF
ANCIENT GREECE

By Alix Wood

PowerKiDS
press

New York

7/16

Published in 2016 by
The Rosen Publishing Group, Inc.
29 East 21st Street, New York, NY 10010

Cataloging-in-Publication Data

Wood, Alix.
Uncovering the culture of ancient Greece / by Alix Wood.
p. cm. — (Archaeology and ancient cultures)
Includes index.
ISBN 978-1-5081-4655-1 (pbk.)
ISBN 978-1-5081-4656-8 (6-pack)
ISBN 978-1-5081-4657-5 (library binding)
1. Greece — History — To 146 B.C. — Juvenile literature. 2. Greece — Civilization — To 146 B.C. —
Juvenile literature. I. Wood, Alix. II. Title.
DF214.W66 2016
938—d23

Editor: Eloise Macgregor
Designer: Alix Wood
Consultant: Rupert Matthews

Photo Credits: Cover, 1 © Dollar Photo Club; 2, 5, 8 bottom, 9 top, 9 bottom right, 11 bottom, 14
bottom, 15 bottom, 17 top, 20, 21 bottom right, 22 top, 23 top, 25 top, 26, 27 top © DollarPhotoClub; 6
© Dreamstime; 7 top © Elisa Triolo; 7 bottom left © Zde/National Archaeological Museum of Athens;
7 bottom right © Katonos Andonis/National Museum Athens; 9 bottom left, 11 middle © Heraklion
Archaeological Museum; 10 top, 23 bottom, 27 © Trustees of the British Museum; 10 bottom ©
Brooklyn Public Library; 12 top © NASA; 12 bottom © Museum of Cycladic Culture, Akrotiri; 13 top ©
Norbert Nagel; 13 middle © Olaf Tausch; 13 bottom © M. M. Taylor; 15 top © National Archaeological
Museum, Athens; 16 top © Pushkin Museum; 16 bottom © Neues Museum, Berlin; 18 top ©
Archaeological Museum of Eretria; 18 bottom © The Hellenic Society; 19 © Dan Diffendale; 21 bottom
left © Harvey Barrison; 22 bottom © James Scott Brown; 24 © Yair Haklai/Delphi Archaeological
Museum; 25 bottom © Delphi Archaeological Museum; 27 middle © Dean Dixon; 29 top © Sarah
Murray; 29 bottom © Corbis Images

Manufactured in the United States of America

CPSIA Compliance Information: Batch #: BW16PK For Further Information contact Rosen Publishing, New York, New York at 1-800-237-9932

CONTENTS

Ancient Greece 4

Sesklo and Dimini 6

Knossos... 8

Code-breaking 10

Volcano! 12

Mycenae... 14

Trojan Treasure 16

Lefkandi.. 18

Valley of the Temples 20

The Home of the Olympics 22

The Oracle.. 24

The Acropolis 26

A Royal Tomb 28

Glossary.. 30

Further Information 31

Index.. 32

ANCIENT GREECE

Ancient Greece is known as "the birthplace of Western civilization." The Greeks created a society that was admired by other countries. The Romans, in particular, were influenced by their art, their **myths**, and their gods. The Ancient Greeks invented a system of **democracy**, and started the Olympic Games. They produced some of history's most intelligent scholars, who wrote about science, art, and thinking.

Ancient Greece was made up of small "**city-states**," each with their own government. Athens, Sparta, and Delphi were important city-states. Sometimes the city-states fought each other, but sometimes they joined together to fight a common enemy, such as Persia.

ANCIENT GREECE

Delphi

Athens

Sparta

TURKEY

Timeline
A colored band by the page number shows each site's time period

c7000-c1600 BCE	c2000 - 1450 BCE	1600 - 1100 BCE	1100 - 800 BCE
Prehistoric	Minoan	Mycenaean	Dark Ages

Artifact Facts

These pots were made by Minoan craftsmen. The Minoans, from the island of Crete, were the first civilization in Greece. The more war-like Mycenaean civilization followed. After the Dark Ages, the Classical Greek period gave rise to most of the art, architecture, and culture the Greeks are famous for.

Minoan pots at Knossos

The Ancient Greeks invented the theater. Most Greek cities had a theater. They were usually outdoor, bowl-shaped arenas on a hillside. At first, Greek theaters were used for music, songs, and dances to honor the Greek gods. The songs told the stories of the gods. Over time the singers began to act out the stories, and Greek writers began to write plays for them to act out.

The theater at Delphi, with a temple to the god Apollo in the background.

800 - 500 BCE	500 - 323 BCE	323 -146 BCE
Archaic Greece	Classical Greece	Hellenistic Greece

SESKLO AND DIMINI

Sesklo Dimini

Two of the earliest human settlements in Greece were the villages of Sesklo and Dimini. The neighboring villages were formed in Neolithic times, just as people started to learn how to farm animals and grow crops. Sesklo was settled around 6,500 BCE, and Dimini around 4,800 BCE.

The people built their villages on hillsides near **fertile** valleys. They grew wheat and barley, and mainly farmed sheep and goats. **Archaeologists** believe the villages must have had leaders, as some houses were significantly bigger than others. The people that lived in the larger houses probably had a higher **status**. Most of the buildings at Sesklo had stone foundations and mud walls, with a timber roof covered with a thick layer of clay. The houses had one or two rooms.

A reconstruction of a Greek mud-brick house at the area's archaeological museum

Dimini had one big house in the center of the village, probably for the village leader. The village also had a total of six protective stone circular walls built around it! The villagers must have been worried about invaders. The walls also had complicated gates to make it hard for an enemy to get in.

In around 4,000 BCE a fire destroyed Sesklo. The fire could have been an accident but some archaeologists believe the town was raided by Dimini!

The ruins of the Neolithic site at Dimini

Sesklo pottery

Artifact Facts

Sesklo people made distinctive pottery which they decorated with red paint (left). The later Dimini pottery was painted with dark brown or black patterns. The pot (right) must have been valued as it was found in an important building at the center of the village.

Dimini pottery

KNOSSOS

CRETE Knossos

Knossos was first inhabited as a Neolithic settlement and later became the capital of the Minoan Civilization in Crete. An early palace, built around 1900 BCE, was destroyed, probably by a large earthquake. The palace was rebuilt and extended but was damaged several times due to earthquakes, invasions, and a nearby volcano that erupted. Knossos was eventually taken over by the invading Mycenaeans who used it as their capital until 1375 BCE.

Arthur Evans

The maze-like building was built on many levels. According to a Greek myth, the palace was designed by the architect, Dedalos, so that no one put in it could find their way out! His employer, King Minos, then kept Dedalos prisoner to keep the exit a secret.

Arthur Evans was a British archaeologist who excavated the site in 1900. He restored large parts of the palace.

The palace's throne room (right) has an **alabaster** seat. If it was a king's throne, it is thought to be the oldest example in Europe. Some archaeologists believe it was actually where a priestess would have sat and performed **rituals**.

The palace ruins at Knossos

Artifact Facts

This beautiful Minoan sculpture of a bull's head is actually a jug! Liquid was poured into the back of the bull's head and came out of its mouth. It was found at the Little Temple at Knossos by Evans.

The Temple of Knossos had an open courtyard area in the center. Some experts believe that the ancient Minoans enjoyed a strange sporting event there. In the temple there are wall paintings of boys and girls somersaulting over the horns of charging bulls! Minoan's believed bulls were **sacred**.

The bull *frieze* at Knossos

CODE-BREAKING

Phaistos

Knossos

Albert Evans unearthed one of the greatest mysteries of archaeology when he found a set of clay tablets at Knossos. The writing on the tablets was in an unknown language, which took three experts and 52 years to solve! The tablets were written in around 1450 BCE in a script Evans called "Linear B." He desperately wanted to decode the text, but died before he was able to. Many years earlier, however, he had visited a school and talked to the children there about his finds. One boy, Michael Ventris, became obsessed with the idea of cracking the Linear B code!

Linear B on a tablet found at Knossos

With the help of American professor, Alice Kober, Ventris eventually did solve the code. Kober sat night after night trying to find patterns in the script that might help find a key. Linear B has about 85 basic characters. Each character probably stood for a sound, like "ma" or "kam." Fewer characters usually means the script is an alphabet, like ours, and more characters usually means each character is a picture of a word.

Alice Kober

Kober noticed several sets words shared similar endings. This information helped Ventris. Sadly, when Kober died in 1950, the code still had not been cracked. In June 1952, Ventris, aged just 29, solved the riddle of Linear B. He noticed the sounds "ko," "no," and "so" and realized they might be a place — Knossos! Ventris started looking for other place names, and began to solve the script.

Evans also found tablets with an even older script on them, which he called "Linear A." Up to now, no one has managed to decode Linear A. Why don't you try?

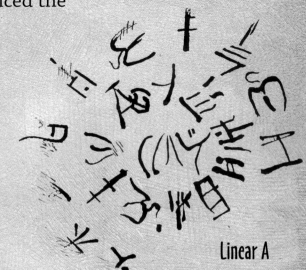
Linear A

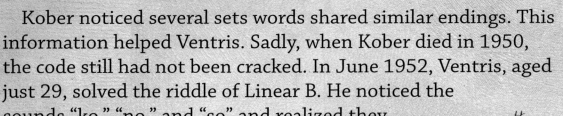

Artifact Facts

Italian archaeologist Luigi Pernier found this dish at Phaistos, in another unknown script. The letters were made by pressing "seals" into soft clay, making it the first "printed" text ever found! Language experts think it is a prayer to a goddess.

The ruins of Phaistos

VOLCANO!

SANTORINI

Akrotiri

The town of Akrotiri was a Minoan Bronze Age settlement on the volcanic Greek island of Santorini. Akrotiri was destroyed by a volcanic eruption in around 1627 BCE and buried in volcanic ash. The ash preserved the remains. In the satellite image below you can just see the top of what remains of the volcano in the center of the huge crater the eruption created.

Akrotiri was a thriving town with paved streets, and a drainage system. The people made high quality pottery and furniture, and created beautiful wall paintings known as **frescoes**.

erupted volcano

Akrotiri

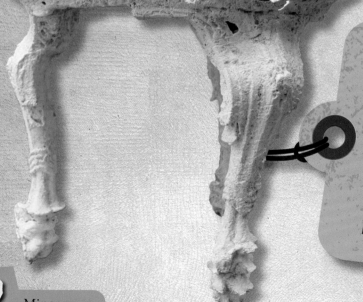

Artifact Facts

This is a plaster cast of a wooden table that was burned away by the volcanic ash, leaving a table-shaped hole behind. Using the hole as a mold, plaster can be poured in and produce entire furniture, in this case a three-legged table!

Archaeologists heard about the buried town of Akrotiri after locals started finding artifacts at a nearby quarry. Greek archaeologist Spyridon Marinatos went to the area. After just a few hours digging he discovered walls. Sadly, Marinatos is actually buried at the site himself, having died while working there some years later.

Archaeologists have found no human remains at the dig, and only a single gold object was found, hidden under a floor. Most of the finds were pottery. This shows that people had some warning to escape the volcano, and quickly took their most valuable things with them.

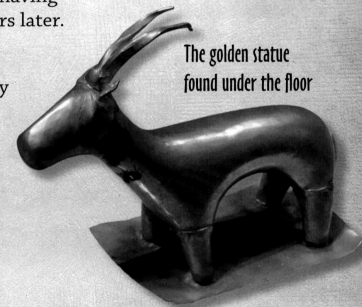

The golden statue found under the floor

One of the beautiful frescoes found at Akrotiri

MYCENAE

Mycenae

Mycenae was one of the major centers of Greek civilization. The period of Greek history from around 1600 BCE to 1100 BCE is called Mycenaean after the city. The city features in the epic stories by the famous poet, Homer.

In 1874, German archaeologist Heinrich Schliemann started exploring the site. At first he started digging there without permission and had to stop! In 1876, he found ancient shaft graves with royal skeletons, and beautiful grave goods. He discovered gold death masks on the skulls of several skeletons.

Heinrich Schliemann

A grave circle at Mycenae

Artifact Facts

When Schliemann discovered this gold mask in one of the grave circles, he sent a telegram to a Greek newspaper, saying, "I have gazed on the face of Agamemnon!" Agamemnon was a king of Mycenae and a famous Greek hero from Homer's stories *The Iliad* and *The Odyssey*.

Some people think that the Mask of Agamemnon is a fake. Schliemann found several other plainer masks in the grave circles. This mask had very obvious differences. The facial hair and the ears cut out from the body of the mask made it different from the others. Because of this some people think that it was not from the same time period, and there is no way to be sure it was actually the grave of Agamemnon himself.

Agamamnon's mask was found in the largest grave circle, known as the Treasury of Atreus (left). The tomb is not thought to be of either Atreus or Agamemnon. Archaeologists believe the man buried there ruled Mycenae before their time. The triangular hole above the door is to reduce the weight of earth over the doorway.

The entrance to the Treasury of Atreus

TROJAN TREASURE

Troy

The Ancient Greeks lived in mainland Greece and the Greek islands. They also ruled coastal areas of what is now Turkey. The ancient city of Troy is in Turkey. The Trojan War with the Greeks was made famous in a long poem, the *Iliad*, by a storyteller named Homer. The prince of Troy ran away with Helen, wife of the king of Sparta. The Greeks sent an army to get her back, and the war lasted for 10 years! In the story, the Greeks won by sneaking soldiers inside a wooden horse which the Trojans allowed into their fortress.

The site at Troy is what archaeologists call a "tell." A tell is an artificial hill, built up out of layers of debris. Each layer is from a different time period. The site has been dug almost constantly since German archaeologist, Heinrich Schliemann, began in 1873. He loved the poems by Homer. Schliemann was very excited to find the site of ancient Troy.

Artifact Facts

When Schliemann discovered treasure at Troy, he believed it belonged to Priam, Troy's king during the Trojan War. Modern archaeologists do not believe this, as it was found in a layer full of artifacts from 1,000 years before his rule.

Some of Priam's treasure

Mycenaean

Some walls and remains of buildings at Troy. In front on the left are two stone wells.

Sophia Schliemann wearing the "Jewels of Helen" excavated by her husband in Troy.

Schliemann **smuggled** Priam's treasure out of Turkey. Officials only noticed when his wife, Sophia, wore the jewels in public! The government stopped Schliemann's dig and **sued** him for its share of the gold. The official assigned to watch the excavation, Amin Effendi, received a prison sentence.

Schliemann traded some treasure for permission to dig at Troy again. The rest of the treasure went to a museum in Berlin, but disappeared when it was hidden in a bunker beneath the Berlin Zoo during World War II. The treasure had been secretly taken to the Soviet Union by the Red Army and was eventually placed in a museum in Moscow.

LEFKANDI

Lefkandi

The Dark Ages in Greece started around 1100 BCE. Much of the country fell into ruin. Palaces were destroyed and the population fell. People were poorer. Little gold jewelry was found from that time, and pots and shoes from the period were badly made. Greece's northern neighbors invaded, and the Greeks fled from many of their cities. Lefkandi was probably settled by the Mycenaeans after they left Knossos. It was a richer village than most Dark Age settlements.

In 1980, archaeologists digging a large mound discovered the remains of a man and woman within an enormous structure believed to be a hero's grave. The ashes of the man were found in a bronze **vessel** engraved with a hunting scene. A sword and other grave goods were nearby. The woman's body was adorned with jewelry. A knife was found near her. Four horses were **sacrificed** and put in the grave, too.

Gold jewelry found on the female body

An area of the vast "hero's grave" at Lefkandi

Artifact Facts

Archaeologists found some fine examples of pottery decorated with pictures, like this one. Unusually for the Dark Ages, archaeologists found many imported objects in the cemetery. The grave of one man, known as the "Warrior Trader" was buried with a wide range of pottery, iron, and bronze artifacts, and a set of trader's balance weights.

A statue of a **centaur** was found by archaeologists in two pieces in two different graves. A centaur has the head of a man and the body of a horse. The head (below) was found among the offerings of one grave, and the body was found in a nearby grave. The Lefkandi centaur is not only an example of early art but also one of the first statues found of a hero from a Greek myth. The Lefkandi centaur is believed to be Chiron, a wise tutor who educated many Greek heroes. There is a gash on the statue's left knee. In a myth about the Greek hero, Herakles, he once wounded Chiron in the knee by mistake.

This statue of Chiron at a grave shows how important myths were in Greek society.

VALLEY OF THE TEMPLES

ITALY

GREECE

Akragas

The Ancient Greeks had colonies all along the coast of the Mediterranean Sea. This territory is known as Magna Graecia, which means "Great Greece" in the Roman language. One of these colonies was in Sicily, an island off the south coast of Italy.

Agrigento, Sicily, is the site of the ancient Greek city of Akragas. Its amazing Valley of the Temples is actually built along a ridge, rather than a valley. Seven enormous Greek temples were built at Akragas in the 6th and 5th centuries BCE. Many have now been excavated and restored. The site is so vast that many more secrets must be buried along the ridge, waiting for archaeologists to discover them.

The Temple of Concordia, one of seven temples at Akragas

One of the atlas statues has been repaired where it lay.

The Temple of Olympian Zeus was the largest **Doric** temple ever built. Today the site is in ruins but at one time the temple was larger than a soccer field! In between its columns were stone figures known as "atlases." These enormous figures helped support the roof. The statues stood with their backs to the wall and hands upstretched above their heads, as if holding up the roof.

Sicilian archaeologist Domenico Antonio Lo Faso Pietrasanta, and later British ex-soldier Alexander Hardcastle worked at separate times excavating the site. Hardcastle spent between 1920 and 1930 looking for an ancient theater. He uncovered walls and ancient roads, and helped restore temples, but found no trace of the theater. He lost all his money when his family's bank collapsed, and died in poverty in Agrigento in 1933.

Artifact Facts
These eight columns from the ruins of the Temple of Heracles were restored by Hardcastle. This statue of Hardcastle stands at Hardcastle's villa next to the temple.

THE HOME OF THE OLYMPICS

Olympia

The Olympic Games started in Olympia over 2,700 years ago. At first, the Games were part of a religious festival held in honor of the god, Zeus. The Games were held every four years. People from all over Greece competed. Because different regions of Greece were sometimes fighting each other, travel could be dangerous. To make sure the Games were well-attended, one month before the Games the organizers announced a time of peace, called the "sacred truce." People could then travel to Olympia in safety!

The gateway to the stadium at Olympia

Part of the starting line at the stadium at Olympia. The track was wide enough for 20 runners to race at once.

At the first Olympic Games, the only event was a race from one end of the stadium to the other! More events were added, such as wrestling, long jump, and chariot racing. Winners were given a **wreath** made of leaves. They would often receive a hero's welcome when they returned home.

The ruins of the Temple of Zeus

The last Games were held at Olympia in 393 CE. Christian emperor Theodosius I then banned what he thought was a **pagan** festival. Earthquakes later destroyed the site. Over time, Olympia was buried under silt from a nearby flooded river.

French archaeologists began work in 1829, discovering the ruins of the Temple of Zeus. The temple had housed the famous statue of Zeus, which was one of the Seven Wonders of the Ancient World! The statue was approximately 43 ft (13 m) high and covered in gold and ivory. Although archaeologists found the temple ruins, there was no trace of the statue. It is believed that wealthy Greeks took the statue to Constantinople and it was destroyed in a fire in 462.

Artifact Facts

Made in Olympia by the sculptor, Phidias, the statue of Zeus took about 12 years to complete. This painting by Alfred Charles Conrade was created from a detailed description of the statue and its throne by Pausanias, a Greek traveler.

THE ORACLE

Delphi

Delphi in the 6th century BCE was the religious center of the ancient Greek world. In myths from the Greek classical period, Zeus sent two eagles flying from the east and west, and the path of the eagles crossed over Delphi. Delphi was therefore believed to be the center of "Grandmother Earth." A temple was built at the center to the god Apollo. If anyone wanted to ask Apollo a question, a priestess, known as the Delphi oracle, would sit on a stool over a crack in the earth and receive a message from Apollo!

Archaeologist John Hale believes Delphi's oracle saw visions because they breathed natural gas that escaped from a crack in the Earth's surface. The escaping gas would make the oracle feel a little strange and they would perhaps say mysterious things. A story says that goatherds first noticed the crack in the Earth when their goats behaved oddly when they wandered nearby!

Artifact Facts

This marble monument was found at Delphi and marked the center of "Grandmother Earth." The stone is called an omphalos. "Omphalos" means "navel" in Greek. The navel was considered the center of the body.

The Temple of
Athena at Delphi

Artifact Facts

This beautiful statue of Antinous was found in July 1893, during the excavations by the archaeologist Théophile Homolle close to the Temple of Apollo. The statue was discovered still standing upright! This photo was taken as the statue was being unearthed.

THE ACROPOLIS

Greece has many mountains, and Greek cities were often built on rocky hills in order to defend themselves more easily. A Greek fortified city built on a hill was called an "acropolis." The most famous is the acropolis in Athens. Athens is named after the Greek goddess Athena. When Pericles ruled Athens it was known as the "golden age" because of the peace and wealth he brought to the city. Most of the great monuments were built at this time.

The Parthenon was built to honor the goddess Athena. It took around fifty years to build. The sculptor, Phidias, created many of the statues and friezes. The Parthenon and other buildings were seriously damaged in 1687 during a siege by the Venetians. The Parthenon was being used for gunpowder storage and exploded after being hit by a cannonball!

These large female statues, known as "caryatids," hold up a porch at one of the temples at the Acropolis. These are copies of the originals, which are now in museums in Greece and Britain.

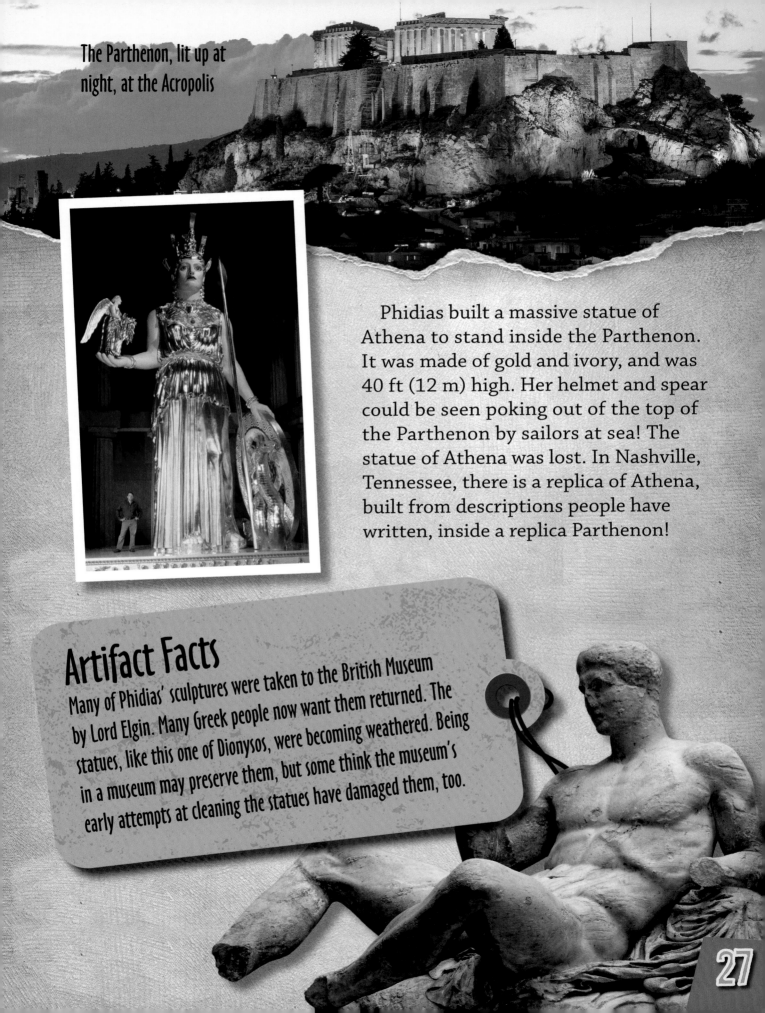

The Parthenon, lit up at night, at the Acropolis

Phidias built a massive statue of Athena to stand inside the Parthenon. It was made of gold and ivory, and was 40 ft (12 m) high. Her helmet and spear could be seen poking out of the top of the Parthenon by sailors at sea! The statue of Athena was lost. In Nashville, Tennessee, there is a replica of Athena, built from descriptions people have written, inside a replica Parthenon!

Artifact Facts

Many of Phidias' sculptures were taken to the British Museum by Lord Elgin. Many Greek people now want them returned. The statues, like this one of Dionysos, were becoming weathered. Being in a museum may preserve them, but some think the museum's early attempts at cleaning the statues have damaged them, too.

27

A ROYAL TOMB

Aigai

French archaeologist, Leon Heuzey, began excavating on a plain south of the Haliacmon River. Heuzey found parts of a large palace, but an outbreak of **malaria** stopped the dig. In 1937, the University of Thessaloniki found more ruins of the ancient palace, but in 1940 the outbreak of war with Italy stopped the excavation. They had found Aigai, the ancient capital of Macedon. It was here, in the theater in 336 BCE that Philip II was **assassinated** and Alexander the Great was proclaimed king.

Greek archaeologist, Manolis Andronikos, believed a hill there called the Great Tumulus hid the tombs of the Macedonian kings. In 1977, he found four buried tombs, two of which had never been disturbed! Andronikos claimed he had found the burial sites of Philip II, father of Alexander the Great, and Alexander IV of Macedon, son of Alexander the Great.

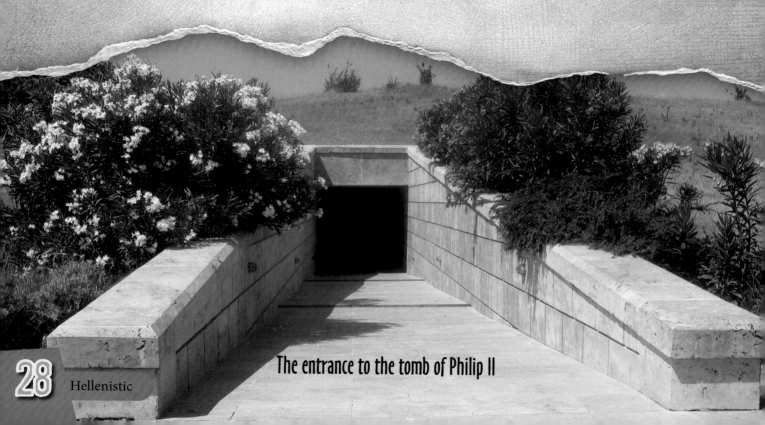

The entrance to the tomb of Philip II

Once inside the entrance passageway, Andronikos discovered this marble doorway (right). Above the door was a painted frieze of a hunt involving men, horses, and dogs. The doors were sealed shut, so the excavators had to enter the tomb by removing a stone in the roof of the chamber. Once inside they found a marble **sarcophagus**.

The marble doorway to the inner tomb

The solid gold chest found in Philip II's tomb

Artifact Facts

Andronikos opened the marble sarcophagus and found this beautiful solid gold chest inside. When he opened the chest, he discovered pieces of **cremated** bones colored purple, and a golden wreath of oak leaves and acorns.

In 2010, experts studied the remains of the cremated bones in the golden chest. They looked at descriptions of the many wounds the king had suffered in battle and matched these to injuries found on the bones. The injuries and the stories matched, leading experts to believe the bones were Philip II's!

GLOSSARY

alabaster A white stone used for carving.

archaeologists Scientists that study past human life, fossils, monuments and tools left by ancient peoples.

assassinated When an important person is murdered, by surprise.

centaur A creature in Greek mythology that is half human and half horse.

city-states A self-governing state consisting of a city and surrounding territory.

cremated Burned a dead body to ashes.

democracy Government by the people.

Doric A simple style of Greek architecture.

fertile Producing vegetation or crops plentifully.

frescoes Painting done on freshly spread moist plaster.

frieze A sculptured or ornamental band around a building.

malaria A disease marked by periodic attacks of chills and fever.

myths Stories often describing the adventures of superhuman beings.

pagan A villager who continued to worship the old gods.

rituals Religious or solemn ceremonies.

sacred Set apart in honor of someone.

sacrificed Offered or killed as a religious sacrifice.

sarcophagus A stone coffin.

smuggled Exported or imported secretly and unlawfully especially to avoid paying taxes.

status A position or rank in relation to others.

sued Having sought justice from a person by bringing a legal action.

vessel A cup or bowl for holding something.

wreath An arrangement of flowers, leaves, or stems fastened in a ring and used for decoration.

FURTHER INFORMATION

Books

Bodden, Valerie. *Greece* (Ancient Civilization).Mankato, MN: The Creative Company, 2014.

Catel, Patrick. *What Did the Ancient Greeks Do for Me?* (InfoSearch: Linking the Past and Present). Chicago, IL: Raintree, 2011.

Doeden, Matt. *Tools and Treasures of Ancient Greece* (Searchlight Books: What Can We Learn from Early Civilizations?). Minneapolis, MN: Lerner Publications, 2014.

Samuels, Charlie. *Technology in Ancient Greece* (Technology in the Ancient World). New York, NY: Gareth Stevens, 2013.

Due to the changing nature of Internet links, PowerKids Press has developed an online list of websites related to the subject of this book. This site is updated regularly. Please use this link to access the list:

www.powerkidslinks.com/ACC/Greece

INDEX

Acropolis, Athens 26, 27
Agamemnon, King 15
Agrigento 20, 21
Aigai 28, 29
Akrotiri 12, 13
Alexander the Great 28
Andronikos, Manolis 28, 29
Antinous 25
Apollo 5, 24
Athena 25, 26, 27
Athens 4
atlas statues 21
Atreus 15
caryatids 26
centaurs 19
Chiron 19
Classical Greece 5
Concordia, Temple of 20
Conrade, Alfred Charles 23
Constantinople 23
death masks 14, 15
Dedalos 8
Delphi 4, 5, 24, 25
Delphi Oracle 24
Dimini 6, 7
Dionysos 27
Effendi, Amin 17
Elgin, Lord 27
Evans, Arthur 8, 9, 10, 11
Hale, John 24

Haliacmon River 28
Hardcastle, Alexander 21
Helen of Troy 16
Heracles, Temple of 21
Herakles 19
Hero's Grave, Lefkandi 18
Heuzey, Leon 28
Homer 14
Homolle, Théophile 25
Iliad, the 15, 16
Knossos 5, 8, 9, 10, 11, 18
Kober, Alice 10, 11
Lefkandi 18, 19
Linear A 11
Linear B 10, 11
Little Temple, Knossos 9
Magna Graecia 20
Marinatos, Spyridon 13
Minoans 5, 8, 9, 12, 13
Minos, King 8
Mycenae 14, 15
Mycenaeans 5, 8, 14, 15, 18
Odyssey, the 15
Olympia 22, 23
Olympian Zeus, Temple of 21
Olympic Games 22, 23
omphalos 24
Parthenon, the 26, 27
Pericles 26

Pernier, Luigi 11
Phaistos 11
Phidias 23, 26, 27
Philip II 28, 29
Pietrasanta, Domenico
    Antonio Lo Faso 21
pottery 7, 19
Santorini 12
Schliemann, Heinrich 14,
    15, 16, 17
Schliemann, Sophia 17
Sesklo 6, 7
Seven Wonders of the
    Ancient World 23
Sicily 20, 21
Sparta 4
Theodosius I 23
Treasury of Atreus,
    Mycenae 15
Trojan War 16
Troy 16, 17
Valley of the Temples 20,
    21
Ventris, Michael 10, 11
Warrior Trader's Grave,
    Lefkandi 19
wells 17
World War II 17
Zeus 22, 24
Zeus, Temple of 23